AMERICA IN THE TIME OF
LEWIS AND CLARK
1801 to 1850

Sally Senzell Isaacs

Heinemann Library
Des Plaines, Illinois

Published by Heinemann Library,
an imprint of Reed Educational & Professional Publishing,
1350 East Touhy Avenue, Suite 240 West
Des Plaines, IL 60018.

973.5
Isaacs

AMERICA IN THE TIME OF LEWIS AND CLARK
was produced for Heinemann Library
by Bender Richardson White.

Editor: Lionel Bender
Designer: Ben White
Assistant Editor: Michael March
Picture Researcher: Madeleine Samuel
Media Conversion and Typesetting: MW Graphics
Production Controller: Kim Richardson

03 02 01 00
10 9 8 7 6 5 4 3

Printed in Hong Kong

Library of Congress Cataloging-in-Publication Data.
Isaacs, Sally, 1950–
     America in the time of Lewis and Clark, 1801 – 1850 / Sally Senzell
Isaacs.
         p.   cm.
     Includes bibliographical references and index.
     Summary: Uses the Lewis and Clark Expedition as a reference to
examine the history and everyday life of the United States from 1801 to
1850, including the War of 1812, the growth of industrialization, the
expansion westward, and the California Gold Rush.
     ISBN 1-57572-744-7 (lib. bdg.) ISBN 1-57572-935-0 (pbk.)
     1. United States--History--1783-1865--Juvenile literature.
2. United States--Social life and customs--1783-1865--Juvenile
literature. 3. Lewis and Clark Expedition (1804-1806)--Juvenile
literature. [1. United States--History--1783-1865. 2. United States--
Social life and customs--1783-1865. 3. Lewis and Clark Expedition
(1804-1806)]   I. Title.
E301.I87   1998
973.5--dc21
                                                         98-34485
                                                            CIP
                                                            AC

Special thanks to Mike Carpenter, Scott Westerfield, and Tristan Boyer at
Heinemann Library for editorial and design guidance and direction.

Photo Credits:
Picture Research Consultants, Mass: pages 13 right (Anne S.K. Brown
Military College), 14 (Slater Mill Historic Site), 26 (Library of Congress),
27 (Library of Congress), 31 (Courtesy of Samuel Herrup Antiques), 34
(Nebraska State Historical Society), 37 (Minnesota Historical Society), 38
(California State Library), 40 (T. W. Wood Gallery), 41 (Courtesy of the New
York Historical Society, New York City). Peter Newark's American Pictures:
pages 6, 8 right, 13 left, 15, 16, 18, 21, 23, 25, 28, 29, 30, 36, 39.
North Wind Pictures: pages 8 left, 11, 19, 22, 33 top, 33 bottom, 35.

Every effort has been made to contact copyright holders of any material
reproduced in this book. Omissions will be rectified in subsequent printings
if notice is given to the publisher.

Artwork credits
Illustrations by: John James on pages 6/7, 8/9, 16/17, 28/29, 34/35;
James Field on pages 12/13, 20/21, 24/25, 40/41; Mark Bergin on
pages 10/11, 18/19, 26/27; Gerald Wood on pages 14/15, 22/23,
32/33, 38/39; Nick Hewetson on pages 30/31, 36/37.
All maps by Stefan Chabluk.
Cover: Design and make-up by Pelican Graphics. Artwork by John James.
Photos: Top: North Wind Pictures. Center: Picture Research Consultants
(Slater Mill Historic Site). Bottom: North Wind Pictures.

Major quotations used in this book come from the
following sources. In some cases, quotes have been
abridged for clarity:
Page 8: Jefferson's instructions to Lewis: *The Journals of
Lewis and Clark*, edited by Bernard DeVoto. New York:
Houghton Mifflin Company, 1953 and 1981, page 481.
Page 10: Clark's journal: *The Journals of Lewis and Clark*,
edited by Bernard DeVoto, New York: Houghton Mifflin
Company, 1953 and 1981, page 256.
Page 12: Madison's speech to Congress. *Documents of
American History*, edited by Henry Steele Commager.
New York: Appleton-Century Crofts, Inc., 1958, page 207.
Page 16: George Catlin quote: *I Have Spoken—American
History through the voices of the Indians*, compiled by
Virginia Irving Armstrong. Chicago: Sage Books, The
Swallow Press, Inc., 1971, page 69.
Page 18: Meeting between Osceola and General
Thompson: From *Native American Testimony*. Edited
by Peter Nabokov. New York: Thomas Y. Crowell,1978,
page 157.
Page 22: Diary of Susan Magoffin. From: *History of US*
by Joy Hakim. New York: Oxford University Press, 1994,
Book 5, page 26.
Page 36: James Polk's address to Congress: From *West
of the West* by Robert Kirsch and William S. Murphy. New
York: E.P. Dutton & Co., Inc. 1967, pages 295-296.
Page 41. Immigrant quotes: *Our Country* (textbook). New
York: Silver Burdett Ginn, 1995, page 404.

The Consultants
Special thanks go to Diane Smolinski and
Nancy Cope for their help in the preparation of
this series. Diane Smolinski has years of
experience interpreting standards documents
and putting them into practice in fourth and
fifth grade classrooms. Nancy Cope splits her
time between teaching high school history,
chairing her department, training new teachers
at North Carolina State University, and being
President-Elect of the North Carolina Council for
Social Studies.

The Author
Sally Senzell Isaacs is a professional writer and
editor of nonfiction books for children. She
graduated from Indiana University, earning a
B.S. degree in Education with majors in
American History and Sociology. For some
years, she was the Editorial Director of
Reader's Digest Educational Division. Sally
Senzell Isaacs lives in New Jersey with her
husband and two children.

August 2001

CONTENTS

ABOUT THIS SERIES

America in the Time of is a series of nine books arranged chronologically, meaning that events are described in the order in which they happened. However, since each book focuses on an important person in American history, the timespans of the titles overlap. In each book, most articles deal with a particular event or part of American history. Others deal with aspects of everyday life, such as trade, houses, clothing, and farming. These general articles cover longer periods of time. The little illustrations at the top left of each article are a symbol of the times. They are identified on page 3.

▼ About the map
This map shows the United States today. It shows the boundaries and names of all the states. Refer to this map, or to the one on pages 42–43, to locate places talked about in this book.

About this book

This book is about America from 1801 to 1850. The term America means "the United States of America." Some historians refer to the native people of America as Indians. Others call them Native Americans, as we do. By 1850, the 13 original colonies had grown into 31 united states. At first, all the western land was wilderness. Then borders were marked and the land became territories, such as Louisiana Territory and Ohio Territory. Once a territory had 60,000 free citizens, it could be admitted as a new state. Words in **bold** are described in more detail in the glossary on page 46.

INTRODUCTION

By the early 1800s, most Americans wanted their country to be as big as possible. Piece by piece, the United States government claimed or purchased land from the Atlantic to the Pacific Oceans.

Meriwether Lewis and William Clark were two brave men assigned to explore America's new land. In a daring expedition, joined by 30 to 40 other explorers, they walked, paddled, and rode horses from St. Louis (now in Missouri) to the Pacific Ocean. They drew maps, took notes, and made friends—and sometimes fought—with Native Americans. Thanks to the work of Lewis and Clark, later explorers and settlers had information about the land, animals, weather, and people of the West.

Some pages in the book tell about the journey of Lewis and Clark. Those pages that describe other events in America include yellow boxes that tell you what Lewis and Clark were doing at the time. Lewis and Clark died before many of the events in this book took place. They never saw wagon trains crossing the Great Plains or mining towns in California. Still, their brave adventures gave other Americans the courage to go west!

As you read this book, use the map on pages 42 and 43 to follow the trails of Lewis and Clark and the Americans who followed them.

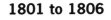

A NEW PRESIDENT

Thomas Jefferson did not ride in the presidential coach. Instead, he rode a horse. He placed his dinner guests at a round table so no one felt more or less important. Thomas Jefferson was a new kind of president. He believed all citizens were equal.

Each New Year's Day and Fourth of July during his presidency, Thomas Jefferson opened the President's House to all Americans who could get there. Rich and poor people were equally welcomed.

Jefferson was different from George Washington and John Adams. He thought the government should not interfere in people's lives. He cut taxes and reduced the size of the **military**. However, like the first two presidents, he worried about the other countries who owned land in North America.

Control of New Orleans

In 1802, the port of New Orleans in Louisiana belonged to France. Americans used this port to send their goods to markets. Farmers from places such as Illinois and Kentucky sent their crops down the Mississippi River to New Orleans, then into the Gulf of Mexico, and up the East Coast. Jefferson was afraid that France might one day stop Americans from using the port.

"Every eye in the United States is now fixed on the affairs of Louisiana," wrote President Jefferson in a letter to Robert Livingston, an American official living in France.

▲ This picture of Thomas Jefferson was painted by Rembrandt Peale in 1800. Thomas Jefferson was born in Virginia in 1743. His father was in Virginia's **House of Burgesses.**

Jefferson grew up on a **plantation**, or large farm, with at least 20 **slaves**. He went to college, became a lawyer, and became very involved in colonial government. He married Martha Wayles Skelton and had six children.

The importance of Thomas Jefferson
Jefferson was known as a good lawyer and a good writer who used plain and simple English. This talent and his love of his country led to these important jobs in the United States:
• wrote the Declaration of Independence
• governor of Virginia
• U.S. official in France
• U.S. **secretary of state**
• vice-president of U.S.
• U.S. president. He became president in March 1801.

The Louisiana Purchase

In 1802, President Jefferson asked Robert Livingston to try to buy New Orleans from the French. He told Livingston to offer $10 million for the city. France's answer surprised them.

France offered to sell all of Louisiana for $15 million! France's ruler, Napoleon Bonaparte, was giving up on the idea of keeping colonies in America. He wanted money for the French army to fight his wars in Europe. Jefferson agreed to the deal. In October 1803, the U.S. **Senate** approved. The United States doubled in size. No one asked the Native Americans who lived in Louisiana if they would agree to the deal.

◀ The Louisiana Purchase moved the **nation**'s western boundary from the Mississippi River to the Rocky Mountains. Later, this land would become these 13 states: Minnesota, Iowa, Missouri, Arkansas, Louisiana, Oklahoma, Kansas, Nebraska, South Dakota, North Dakota, Montana, Wyoming, Colorado.

◀ Flags are changed in New Orleans in 1803 to mark the Louisiana Purchase. At this ceremony, the French flag is taken down and the American "Stars and Stripes" flag is raised.

LEWIS AND CLARK

Thomas Jefferson had hundreds of questions about his Louisiana Purchase. Was it a bargain or a bust? Was the land good for farming? Were the Native Americans friendly or warlike? Was there a way to cross the Rocky Mountains? Was there a major waterway to the Pacific Ocean?

Jefferson called in his private secretary, Meriwether Lewis. He knew that Lewis had served in the army on the **frontier.** He asked Lewis to consider leading a group of explorers through the rivers of the Louisiana **Territory.** Lewis wrote to his friend, William Clark, to ask him to join the group. Both men said yes.

Jefferson wrote instructions to Lewis. He wanted Lewis and Clark to bring back maps and written notes about: "the soil and face of the country...the animals of the country, generally, and especially those not known in the U.S...the mineral production of every kind...climate as characterized by...proportion of rainy, cloudy and clear days...the dates at which particular plants put forth or lose their flowers...times of appearance of particular birds, reptiles, or insects."

Getting ready to go
Lewis and Clark were good partners because they were not alike. Lewis was shy and moody. He liked science and studying nature. Clark was cheerful and liked chatting with people. He was good at drawing maps.

Lewis and Clark spent months preparing for their trip. They:
• practiced scientific methods for gathering seeds
• learned how to draw and identify animals
• studied Native American culture
• trained other men for the journey. Many of the group knew Native American languages.

▲ Lewis and Clark's largest boat was a keelboat like this one. It was 55 feet (17 m) long with a square sail and 22 oars for rowing.

▲ Two canoes accompanied the keelboat. One canoe had six oars, the other seven. Fifty men started on the trip.

Patrick Gass, a member of the expedition, drew this picture of a meeting with Sioux Native Americans in Iowa.

By May, 1805, the explorers have traveled the Missouri River to a narrowing in the Milk River (in present-day Montana). Lewis points out features of the land and water. Clark draws a map. A man named York is seated on the rock. He is Clark's **slave**. The team depends on his excellent hunting and fishing skills. Because of his dark skin, Native Americans trust him.

When the explorers reached North Dakota in the winter of 1804, they met Sacagawea. She helped them communicate with Native Americans.

The explorers had a well-equipped medicine chest with more than 20 remedies.

As a symbol of friendship, Lewis and Clark gave Peace and Friendship Medals like these to Native American chiefs. The chiefs proudly wore the gifts on ribbons around their necks.

On May 14, 1804, Lewis and Clark's team of explorers gathered at the Missouri River near St. Louis. They loaded these supplies onto their three boats: clothing, tools, guns, food, and medical supplies. They also brought things to trade with the Native Americans: beads, ribbons, American flags, fish hooks, and needles.

As the team started their journey, settlers from villages along the river cheered from the shore. Days later, there were no more villages. The explorers reached the quiet wilderness of unsettled territories.

DISCOVERIES

William Clark's journal, October 19, 1805: "I observed a great number of lodges on the opposite side [of the Columbia River]...and several Indians on the opposite bank....They returned to their lodges as fast as they could run. They said we...were not men."

Clark approached the lodge with small trinkets and a peace pipe. The Native Americans were still frightened. Then Clark's Native American guide, Sacagawea, entered the lodge. Soon everyone relaxed and realized that the explorers were friendly. Lewis and Clark appreciated the help of the Native Americans they met. They taught them where the rivers and waterfalls were and which animals and plants to eat.

Some highlights of the expedition

Spring 1804: They are hit by a violent tornado followed by "troublesome mosquitoes." *Summer 1804:* They observe pelicans, prairie dogs, and buffalo. *Winter 1804:* They build a sturdy log fort outside a Mandan tribal village and wait out the bad weather. *Spring 1805:* The Great Falls of the Missouri River is ahead. The explorers bury a canoe and some supplies. They build wooden carts to push their other canoes and supplies over land. The keelboat is sent back to St. Louis.

▶ Lewis and Clark set out from St. Louis on May 14, 1804. They traveled up the Missouri River in boats. Then they acquired horses from the Shoshone and crossed the Rocky Mountains. On November 7, 1805, they reached the Pacific Ocean. They built a winter camp, Fort Clastop. In the spring of 1806, they set off for home.

A round trip of 7,700 miles (12,392 km)

The team took 1 year, 5 months, and 24 days to reach the Pacific Ocean. Eager to share their news and spending less time investigating, they made the return trip in just 6 months.

On their return journey, Lewis and Clark split up to try to find a shorter route over the Rocky Mountains. Lewis led a group directly east to the Missouri River. Clark almost retraced his steps, then followed the Yellowstone River to the Missouri.

Lewis and Clark reunited in August 1806 and returned to St. Louis.

◀ As the explorers crossed the **Great Plains**, they saw wild animals unfamiliar to them. They saw groups of prairie dogs (far left) that made their homes under the ground. They estimated that they saw 3,000 buffalo.

▲ Lewis and Clark shoot a grizzly bear, previously unknown to white people. This woodcut is by Patrick Gass of the expedition.

◀ On August 17, 1805, the explorers met with the Shoshone leader, Great Chief Chameahwait. The chief turned out to be Sacagawea's brother. The chief gave the explorers horses. He also gave advice about crossing the Rockies.

▼ This is what Clark's drawing of a sage grouse discovered by Lewis on June 5, 1805, looked like.

To the Pacific Ocean

Summer 1805: The river gets too shallow for canoes. They use horses to cross the Rocky Mountains. *Fall 1805:* On the far side of the Rockies, they build canoes and follow the Columbia River to the Pacific! *Spring 1806:* Start homeward.

Lewis and Clark collected a wealth of information about the newest part of the United States. For years after, settlers followed their trails.

THE WAR OF 1812

In 1806, when Lewis and Clark returned from the Pacific Ocean, France and Great Britain were at war again. The leader of France was trying to take over Great Britain. Americans were suffering from this war even though they lived thousands of miles away.

American merchants had been trading with both Britain and France. Suddenly, both countries said they would capture any ships that traded with their enemy. American ships were captured by both sides. Then the British forced American sailors to fight in the British navy. Americans were outraged at the British.

The war of poor communications
Communications were very slow in the early 1800s. There were no telegraphs, phones, or radios. Messages were taken by horse, train, or ship. On June 16, 1812, Britain promised to stop bothering American ships. The news did not reach America in time. On June 18, President James Madison asked **Congress** to declare war on Britain.

For over two years, America and Britain fought many battles in Canada. Finally, on December 24, 1814, **representatives** of the two countries signed a peace **treaty** in Ghent, Belgium. Again, news did not reach America in time. Fifteen days later, the war's bloodiest battle took place in New Orleans.

The War of 1812 was unusual in U.S. history: It did not have a winner. Each country gave back the land it captured.

Lewis and Clark move on
In 1807, Meriwether Lewis became governor of the Louisiana Territory. He died in 1809. William Clark became governor of the Missouri Territory in 1813.

▼ America won its first battle on the waters of Lake Erie. On September 10, 1813, Commodore Oliver Perry's nine ships defeated Britain's six ships. Here, a British ship is being attacked. America won control of the lake and captured much of upper Canada.

Events in the war
June 1812 U.S. declares war on Great Britain
September 1813 U.S. wins Battle of Lake Erie
August 1814 British burn the President's House (now called the White House) and Capitol in Washington, D.C.
December 1814 Treaty of Ghent ends War of 1812
January 1815 U.S. wins Battle of New Orleans.

Meanwhile
In 1808, Congress passed a new law. **Slaves** could no longer be brought into the United States. But people could still buy slaves from other American slaveowners.

▲ Tecumseh was a Shawnee leader. He brought eastern Native Americans together to fight for their land. Tecumseh volunteered his people to help the British in the war. He was killed in battle by an American soldier on October 5, 1813, as shown in this 1840s **lithograph**.

▲ This **engraving** was made by an unkown artist in 1815 and is called Capture of City of Washington. The White House was only 14 years old when the British attacked Washington, D.C. and set the building on fire. Then they attacked Baltimore, in Maryland.

FACTORIES

In 1813, a Boston merchant named Francis Lowell visited England's cloth factories. He saw large machines making hundreds of yards of cotton cloth which were then shipped to America. "Why couldn't America make its own cloth?" he wondered.

◀ An **engraving** of inside a cotton mill of 1815.

New states and colonies of America
1803 Ohio **statehood**
1816 Indiana statehood
1817 Mississippi statehood
1818 Illinois statehood
1819 Alabama statehood
1819 U.S. buys Florida from Spain
1820 Maine statehood
1821 Missouri statehood
1821 Stephen Austin starts an American colony in Mexico's Texas.

▶ In this cotton-mill factory town:
1. wagons bring raw cotton to the factory
2. a water wheel powers the machines
3. spinning machines turn cotton into thread and wind it around bobbins
4. weaving machines weave threads into cloth.

14

Francis Lowell returned to America, and in 1814 built a cotton processing factory in Waltham, Massachusetts, not far from Boston. There were many machines in the factory. Some machines spun cotton into thread. Others wove the thread into cloth. The factory was built next to the Charles River. The rushing water powered a water wheel, which powered the machines.

The first women factory workers

After Lowell's death in 1817, his business partners built a factory town, called Lowell, in Massachusetts. They built factories, stores, churches, and **boarding-houses** for the employees. Many of the workers were teenage women from farms who had never been able to find full-time paid work before. They worked in the factories until they decided to marry.

▲ Lowell's factories processed raw cotton from **plantations** in the South. This **engraving** from 1800 shows a plantation owner selling his cotton to a factory owner. Black **slaves** operate a cotton gin, which separated cotton fibers from the seeds.

▲ Children who worked in the factories were often told to get behind machines to fix broken threads. This was a dangerous job.

A changing world

Factory workers worked 12 hours a day, 6 days a week. Most workers were women and children. While parents stayed on their farms, sons and daughters worked in the factory towns. Cities grew around the factories. Then people started moving from farms to cities. This was the start of America's Industrial **Revolution**.

THE U.S. ARMY VS. THE SEMINOLES

"Friends and Brothers: I come from your great father, the President of the United States....On the 9th of May, 1832, you entered into a treaty at Payne's Landing...you must prepare to move by the time the cold weather shall have passed away."

These were the words of U.S. General Wiley Thompson at a meeting with some Seminole chiefs on October 23, 1834. From 1832 to 1834, the government had signed **treaties** with Seminole chiefs in Florida. The chiefs had agreed to leave the land. In exchange, they would get new land in Oklahoma, as well as cattle and money.

Yet many Seminoles refused to honor the treaty. Chief Osceola was one of them. He spoke up at this meeting with General Thompson: "My Brothers! The white people got some of our chiefs to sign a paper to give our lands to them, but our chiefs did not do as we told them to do. The agent tells us we must go away from the lands we live on—our homes, and the graves of our Fathers, and go over the big river [the Mississippi] among the bad Indians. When the agent tells me to go from my home, I hate him, because I love my home and will not go from it."

> **Three Seminole Wars**
> The Seminoles and the United States Army fought each other in:
> **1817–1818** The British, who claimed Florida, encouraged the Seminoles to fight American settlers.
> **1835–1842** The U.S. Army forced Seminoles to move west.
> **1855–1858** Remaining Seminoles fought to stay on their land, then agreed to move west.

▶ The Seminoles prepare to **ambush** American soldiers who have arrived at one of Florida's swamplands. The Seminoles know the area well so they can hide among the swampy islands. The soldiers must wade through tall grasses just to find their enemy.

▲ At the same time, Cherokees who survived the Trail of Tears built log cabins like this one to live in.

▶ This picture of Seminole chief Osceola was painted by George Catlin in about 1835. In 1837, Osceola raised a white flag, asking for a truce. In the rules of war, when one side raises a white flag, both sides stop fighting and have a meeting. Instead, U.S. General Thomas Jesup had his troops hidden around the meeting place. When Osceola arrived, he was captured. He died in jail of malaria in 1838.

◀ St. Augustine in Florida is the oldest permanent European settlement in the United States. It was founded by Spain in 1565. This woodcut shows a Spanish presidio (fort) during the days when Spain owned Florida. In 1821, Florida became a **territory** of the United States. Even today, St. Augustine has many historic Spanish buildings.

A long, costly battle

In 1835, President Andrew Jackson sent the U.S. army to Florida to move out the Seminoles. The Seminoles hid in the swamps, refusing to leave. Bitter fighting continued for seven years. Runaway **slaves** who were hiding in Florida helped the Seminoles fight. When the war ended in 1842, the United States had lost 1,500 soldiers and $20 million. In 1835, there had been 5,000 Seminoles living in Florida. By 1842, 400 had been killed, 4,000 had moved to Indian Territory, and only 600 were left.

◀ Both the U.S. army and the Seminoles had guns and rifles. But the Seminoles had fewer weapons and fewer warriors. In addition, the Seminole leaders often could not agree on their battle plans.

19

WINNING LAND FROM MEXICO

Between 1820 and 1830, many Americans left their homes and wrote the letters GTT on their doors. The letters stood for "Gone to Texas." In those years, about 25,000 Americans went to settle in Texas, a territory of Mexico. The Mexican government was giving away land to settlers who would build farms there.

By 1830, the Mexican government was afraid of the Americans in Texas. Many new settlers refused to obey Mexican laws. That year, Mexico stopped allowing Americans into Texas. In October 1835, Texans—led by Samuel Houston—began to fight for Texas's independence from Mexico.

One of the most famous battles was the Battle of the Alamo, a fort in San Antonio. About 200 Texans tried to hold back the Mexican army of 5,000 soldiers led by General Antonio Lopéz de Santa Anna. Fighting lasted for 12 days. Fifteen hundred Mexican soldiers were killed. The Texans lost the battle. All the Texas soldiers in the Alamo were killed.

▶ This is a battle scene from the Mexican War in 1846. Most of the battles took place in present-day Mexico, California, and Texas. Many Americans and President James Polk wanted to add the region called the Mexican Cession to the United **States**. This included California, Nevada, Utah, and parts of Wyoming, New Mexico, Colorado, and Arizona.

Texas history
1821 End of Spanish rule. Americans begin to settle Texas, now part of Mexico.
1835 The Texas **Revolution** begins
1836 Texas wins independence from Mexico
1845 Texas becomes the 28th state
1846 War between Mexico and U.S. begins
1848 U.S. gains **territory** called the Mexican Cession
1853 U.S. buys Gadsden Purchase from Mexico

RED RIVER BASIN 1818
OREGON 1846
LOUISIANA 1803
MEXICAN CESSION 1848
USA 1783
TEXAS 1845
GADSDEN PURCHASE 1853
FLORIDA 1819

◀ This map shows when the United States gained more land from 1783 to 1853.

The Republic of Texas

Sam Houston gathered more Texas soldiers. On April 21, 1835, they surrounded Santa Anna's troops at San Jacinto, Texas. The Mexicans were quickly crushed and Santa Anna was forced to give Texas its independence. Texas was an independent **nation** for nearly 10 years. It had its own **constitution** and president, Samuel Houston. In 1845, it joined the United States to gain government help.

Another war with Mexico

The United States and Mexico still argued about the Texas **boundary.** In 1846, U.S. president James Polk declared war on Mexico. After nearly two years of battles, the United States won. Mexico sold Utah, California, Nevada, and parts of Arizona, New Mexico, Colorado, and Wyoming for $15 million. Finally in 1853, the U.S. bought the Gadsden Purchase from Mexico for $10 million. It included southern Arizona and New Mexico.

◀ This picture of the Battle of the Alamo was painted by Robert Onderdonk in 1905. **Pioneer** Davy Crockett is at the center of a group of Texans holding back the Mexican soldiers at the Alamo. This building was a Spanish **mission** used as a fort by Texans. On March 6, 1835, the Texans lost the battle. Some historians say Davy Crockett was killed at the Alamo. Others say he was taken as a prisoner and then killed.

AMERICA MOVES WEST

"There is such independence, so much free uncontaminated air. I breathe free without that oppression and uneasiness felt in the gossiping circles of a settled home." Susan Magoffin, a pioneer woman, wrote these words in her diary. Her family was going west in 1846—like thousands of other Americans.

▼The National Road, the main road west, went from Maryland to Illinois. Here, a stagecoach leaves an inn where passengers, driver, and horses have rested.

Filled with hopes and dreams, Americans headed west. They walked, rode horses, sailed boats, and rode in wagons. They were called **pioneers** because they were new people coming to a land to prepare it for others. They came from the eastern **states** in the North and the South. Some crossed the ocean from Europe before joining groups heading west.

Pioneers were usually looking for land to own and farm. Land in the East was expensive, but out West it was cheap. Before the 1840s, most pioneers traveled as far west as Illinois or Missouri. After 1840, they went to Oregon and California.

▼ Heading west, this family loaded their wagon and animals onto a flatboat and traveled down a river.

▲ Along the river shores of Kentucky, Tennessee, Indiana, Illinois, and Missouri, pioneers took their flatboats apart and used the wood to build a temporary shelter. Later they would build log cabins.

▼ ▶ Pioneers chopped trees and stacked them to make walls for their cabins. Spaces between the logs were filled in with moss, clay, or mud. After the roof and fireplace were built, pioneers set split logs into the ground to make a wooden floor.

▲ A religious group, the Mormons, first lived in western New York, then in Ohio, Missouri, and Illinois. They were always forced to leave by neighbors who did not agree with their belief in sharing everything. Their leader, Brigham Young, led them west to the Great Salt Lake in present-day Utah. There, in 1847, they set up a new community.

Working together to get settled

The pioneers usually arrived in the spring, in time to clear the land and plant crops. Neighbors helped each other to clear out rocks, chop trees, move logs, and build cabins. A typical log cabin had one room, measuring about 16 by 20 feet (5 by 6 m). Often there was a raised loft for the children's sleeping space.

A family started its new life with perhaps only some kitchen pots and a chair. It built its own tables and benches from logs. It carved its own wooden spoons and bowls and made its own candles and soap. **Peddlers** traveled through new settlements selling some items. As the settlement grew, stores were opened by blacksmiths and other craftworkers.

THE ERIE CANAL

Factories sprung up in New York, Massachusetts, and Pennsylvania. Cities grew around the factories. By 1825, people were thinking about a better way to transport people and goods. A horse-drawn carriage could move only a small load. A boat in the ocean, on a river, or on the Great Lakes could carry much more.

▼ Many **pioneers** started their journey on the Erie Canal. Then they traveled overland, forming a **wagon train** to go west. Meanwhile, in the East the first railroads were being built.

For 100 years, people had talked about building a waterway to connect the Great Lakes to the Atlantic Ocean. In 1812, a man named DeWitt Clinton had a plan to build a canal to do just that. A canal is a waterway dug through the land. At first, many people laughed at Clinton's idea. They called it "Clinton's Ditch." In 1816, Clinton finally received money from the New York state government. A giant eight-year building project began. On October 26, 1825, the Erie Canal opened.

Faster and cheaper transportation
Hundreds of boats could now travel between Buffalo on Lake Erie to Albany on the Hudson River. Goods were moved by cargo boats. Travelers could pay $1\frac{1}{2}$ cents a mile (1.6 km) and ride a slow boat, going 2 mph (3.2 km/hr). Or, they could pay 5 cents a mile and travel 4 mph (6.4 km/hr). Either way, canals were better than roads.

Villages along the 360-mile-long (576 km) canal, such as Utica, Syracuse, Rochester, and Buffalo, grew into big towns. New York City on the Hudson River became the country's largest city. When the Erie Canal proved successful, other canals were built in Virginia and Illinois.

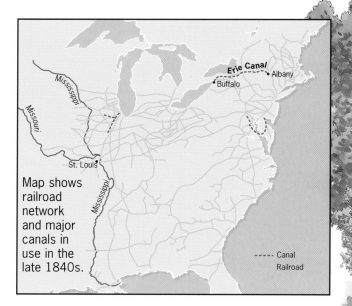

Map shows railroad network and major canals in use in the late 1840s.

- - - - - Canal
———— Railroad

▲ Seven million Europeans—mostly from Germany, Scandinavia, and Ireland—came to America between 1820 and 1870. Many of these **immigrants** stayed in New York City. Others helped build the Erie Canal or joined wagon trains going west.

◀ Many factories were built in America. By the mid-1800s, coal was the best source of energy for running factory machines. Many people had jobs as coal **miners** in Pennsylvania. This job was dangerous as mine shafts often collapsed.

▲ It took eight years and thousands of workers to build the Erie Canal. With only human and horse power, it was an unbelievably tough job to dig through the hills of New York State, as here at Lockport. The canal was 40 feet wide and 4 feet deep (12 m by 1.2 m). Horses and mules pulled boats through the canal. The animals walked on a path next to the water.

◀ Cutting wood with steam-powered machines first occurred about 1830. Plenty of wood was needed to build canal boats, ocean-going ships for international trade, and warehouses, stores, and houses in America's growing cities.

25

MOVING FASTER

Americans were ready for faster transportation. People living in the West needed farming supplies from factories in the East. Factories in the East needed cotton from the South and lumber and food from the West. Wagons and flatboats were too small and slow. Along came boats and trains that ran on steam power.

In 1807, Robert Fulton invented a steamboat. It could travel at a speed of 5 mph (8 km/hr). Within a few years, Fulton's boats were traveling 10 mph (16 km/hr). The first steamboats burned wood. Later, they burned coal. By 1860, there were about 1,000 steamboats chugging through America's rivers and Great Lakes.

In 1830, Peter Cooper built a steam locomotive that could pull a train 18 mph (29 km/hr). At first, people were nervous about riding trains. Would the smoky boiler blow up? Would the speeding train hurtle off the tracks? But by 1850, railroads were becoming America's most important form of transportation. They could carry large loads over long distances. Trains were traveling 28 mph (45 km/hr), while canal boats traveled 4 mph (6.4 km/hr).

Railroads had other advantages over canals. Railroad tracks could be built almost anywhere, not just through flat land. In addition, many canals froze in the winter and could not be used. By 1860, America stopped using canals for mass transportation.

▲ America's first steam-powered locomotive arrived from Stourbridge, England, in May 1829. People called it the *Stourbridge Lion*. The locomotive successfully made its first run in Honesdale, Pennsylvania.

▶ By 1850, New Orleans had become one of America's great ports. Here steamboats on the Mississippi River unload cotton brought from the North. Oceangoing ships transported the cotton to factories on the East Coast.

In the mid-1800s, thousands of **slaves** moved from southern **states** to northern states. They were escaping to the North where slavery was against the law. This picture shows slaves rushing from a boat to covered wagons on their way to freedom.

People called **abolitionists** helped the runaway slaves. In 1850, a law was passed to allow owners to capture slaves in the North and send them back South. That is why many runaway slaves went on to Canada. Their secret escape routes and hiding places were called the Underground Railroad.

In 1832, Cyrus McCormick invented a machine called a reaper that helped farmers cut wheat in the fields. This speeded up harvesting. Horses pulled the reaper. McCormick sold his reapers to farmers all over the country.

US MAIL PACKET

Steamboats like this one had paddlewheels powered by steam engines. They could travel up and down rivers. Flatboats could only float in the direction of the river flow. Steamboats carried cargo and passengers.

Wealth from the Seas

"The skipper's on the quarter deck, a-squinting at the sails. When up aloft the lookout sights a school of spouting whales." This was part of the song "Blow Ye Winds." It was sung by whalers who left from small New England villages and sailed the world's oceans in search of great whales.

Whalers had a dangerous job. They might get injured or killed working the sails or their ship might get destroyed by a whale or wrecked in a storm. Yet it was an exciting and profitable job. By the 1820s, there was great demand for whale oil. Whale oil was made by cutting off the fat under the whale's skin and boiling it. People burned whale oil for light. Fat from one whale could light all the lamps of a small town for many months.

Many whalers lived in seaside villages in Massachusetts and Connecticut. They left their homes and families, sometimes for three or four years, to live aboard whaling ships and travel the oceans. If they were lucky, they would return with many barrels of valuable whale oil and other useful whale parts. The killing, cutting, boiling, and packing were all done at sea.

From 1820 to 1850, over 10,000 whales were killed. Whales were in danger of becoming **extinct**. By 1865, the need for whale oil dropped as people began using **kerosene** and then electricity.

▲ Whale oil was burned for light. Whalebone, or baleen, was made into stiffeners for **corsets**. Other parts of the whale were made into candles and perfume. The teeth were carved into jewelry.

▼ This picture, published in 1852, shows a whale destroying a boat. On seeing a whale, the whalers got into smaller boats and rowed closer to throw their **harpoons** at the whale. Since ropes joined the harpoons to the boat, the whale dragged the boat along until it tired out or died.

◀ The best whaling grounds were in the Pacific Ocean. San Francisco was a major whaling port, as in this painting of 1850.

▶ Whalers' wives stood on their balconies to watch for the return of their husbands' ships.

▼ As barrels of whale oil came off the ship, clerks took notes. Other important jobs in a whaling village were:
• lumber cutter
• shipbuilder
• barrelmaker
• ropemaker
• sailmaker
• carpenter
• blacksmith
• innkeeper
• shopowner.

29

THE BIG CITY

America was beginning to change from a nation of farms to a nation of cities. While pioneers were interested in wide-open spaces, city people did not seem to mind a crowd. Nearly a million people lived in New York City in 1850. Philadelphia, Boston, Cincinnati, and New Orleans were other big cities.

Many farmers moved to the city to escape the long hours and loneliness of farming. They took city jobs in factories, stores, and offices. **Immigrants** also moved to the cities to find jobs. Most of them came from Europe to escape wars, **famines**, and poverty in their homelands.

Cities were exciting places. Newspapers were published every day and sold for only a penny. Department stores were more than two stories high and sold many kinds of things in one building. They even had big show windows in front. Cities also had hotels, theaters, museums, and concert halls. Americans were proud of their cities.

▶ In cities, shoppers, passers-by, business people, and horse-drawn carriages and wagons mingled on the streets.

▶ One of the most run-down and dangerous areas of New York City was called Five Points. Five streets crossed at one intersection. Today, this area is part of the financial district of Manhattan. In this picture of 1829, the streets are filled with people shopping, **peddlers**, and horse-drawn carriages, as well as people fighting.

▼ This picture shows Manhattan Island, part of New York City. Stores in Manhattan sold food, household items, and the lastest fashions from Europe. Before the streets were paved, city shopping was a dirty business. On dry days, carriages kicked up dirt; on rainy days, the streets turned to mud.

◄ Most city buildings were made of wood. Fires were a great danger. New York City had a terrible fire in the winter of 1835. The city's volunteer fire fighters raced to the scene in their horse-drawn fire wagons, but the water in the hydrants was frozen. Most of the city—700 buildings—burned to the ground.

◄▼ Fire fighters used leather buckets and leather protective hats like those shown here.

Communications
In 1844, the telegraph was invented and America had its first long-distance communication service. Messages were put into a code of electrical signals and sent along wires. The wires were suspended from wooden poles. At the receiving end, an operator wrote out the translated messages. Eventually, the whole country would be criss-crossed with wires.

Bad housing, crime, and garbage

As cities grew, so did their problems. There was not enough housing. Poor people crowded into run-down buildings. Some poor people made shelters, called shanties, from pieces of cardboard or wood. Most cities did not have police forces. Along with hard-working people came robbers and pickpockets.

One of the worst city problems was dirt and germs. Cities had no garbage collectors. They depended on hogs, dogs, and birds to eat the garbage. There were no sewer systems to get rid of human wastes. Waste water from toilets, baths and sinks often went into open street gutters. Disease spread quickly. Cities slowly began to take care of their health problems, but not until 1900.

LIFE ON A WAGON TRAIN

They called it Oregon Fever. Thousands of people packed their belongings in covered wagons and went west. They had heard stories about wheat growing 6 feet (1.8 m) high and land enough to make everyone rich. The 6-month trip took them 2,000 miles (3,200 km) from home, across prairies, deserts, and the Rockies.

"Those who crossed the plains never forgot the...craving hunger and utter physical exhaustion of the trail, and the rude crosses which marked the last resting places of loved companions. Neither would they ever forget the...sunrise in the mountains; the campfire at night...and the pure sweet air of the desert."

A writer named Octavius T. Howe wrote about going west on an 1840s **wagon train**. **Pioneers** needed to travel together. Only the guide in front knew the route. At night the wagons formed a circle to keep out wild animals or attacks from Native Americans who resented the disruption to their lands.

► This engraving of the 1850s by W.H. Cary shows pioneers traveling west.

▼ This is a reconstruction of a trading post at Fort Laramie, Wyoming, where pioneers could buy cooking equipment.

Timing the journey carefully

Before setting out, families met in a "jumping-off town" such as Independence, Missouri. They started their journey in May, when there was grass along the trail for their animals. If they left too late, they would not make it over the Rocky Mountains by the first snowfall in October.

From 1840 to 1860, over 300,000 people made the journey to Oregon or California. Most pioneers traveled the Oregon Trail. During the summer months, the trail was dry and dusty. Rain turned the trail to mud. Wagon wheels broke. Animals died. Still, the pioneers had to keep on the move. Those that had to cross the Rocky Mountains in the winter usually died.

▲ A wagon train was a group of covered wagons that traveled west together. Usually, there were set trails to follow. Small children and their mothers rode in the wagons. So did the injured and sick. Men rode horses. Everyone else walked, keeping an eye on the pioneers' cattle, dogs, and chickens.

Wagons were called "prairie schooners." From a distance, their white canvas tops looked like sails on a ship. Oxen or mules pulled the wagons. The wagon train traveled 15 to 20 miles (24 to 32 km) a day. The trip to Oregon took between 4 and 6 months.

▲ Families took only their most important possessions, such as clothing, pots and pans, guns, saws, and axes. However, if the wagon broke or an ox died, these possessions were left on the side of the trail to lighten the load.

▲ All pioneers brought along their cooking utensils. The family chickens laid eggs and the cows provided milk. Men hunted antelope for steaks and prairie-chicken for stews. Pioneers cooked their meals over a campfire or under hot coals.

HOUSES IN THE GREAT PLAINS

Many pioneers did not go all the way to Oregon. They made their homes in the Great Plains. This grassy prairie land was good for growing corn, wheat, and potatoes, and for raising cattle, pigs, and sheep. The Great Plains also had wild thunderstorms, freezing winters, beastly hot summers—and Native Americans.

▲ The Great Plains is a huge area of dry grassland. It is now a major agricultural and mining region.

Pioneers arrived in the **Great Plains** with little money. Most likely, they spent their savings on the wagon and oxen that brought them there, or on rifles and guns to protect themselves from the Native Americans, who had been moved out. Land was cheap, but everything else was very expensive because it had to be transported a long way.

Few trees grew on the plains, so only rich people could afford log cabins. Most people built sod houses, which were made of hard-packed earth and mud. Pioneers cut "sods"—slabs of grassy earth—and stacked them to make walls. Roofs were also made of earth, laid on top of wooden poles. Grass grew on the roof. Snakes, rats, and bugs lived in that grass and they also fell into the house.

Cooking and preserving food

Food was prepared on a cast-iron stove. Corn was brought in from the fields and made part of almost every meal. Pioneers ate several kinds of corn bread, such as corn pone, johnnycake, and hoecake. They also ate corn on the cob.

Pioneers ate meat, too. Since there were no refrigerators, they found other ways to keep meat from spoiling. They smoked it over a fire, dried it in the sun, or soaked it in salty water. Then the meat stayed good for several months.

▶ Sod houses had no running water. A toilet was in a wooden shelter outside the house. It was a simple hole in the ground.

▶ This is an early photograph of pioneers outside their sod house in Nebraska. On a mound above the house, horses pull a wagonload of sods needed to repair the roof. The house is built like those of the Mandan and Pawnee **tribes** who lived in the area.

◀ Farmers used a special "sod-buster" plow to break the tough grass roots. This ox-drawn steel plow was developed by John Deere in 1837.

▼ A family of seven lives in this sod house. The stove in the corner is used for heat and cooking. For fuel, these people burn dried buffalo dung, called "buffalo chips." They carry water from a 100-foot-deep (30 m) well they have dug on their farm.

▲ Most pioneers built their own houses, but they often bought the doors and windows by mail order. They picked up their delivery at the nearest **trading post**.

CALIFORNIA GOLD RUSH

In January 1848, John Marshall was working at John Sutter's sawmill near Sacramento, California. He noticed something sparkling beneath his feet. It was gold! Soon the words "Gold at Sutter's Mill!" were being heard around the world.

On December 5, 1848, President James Polk told **Congress**: "Nearly the whole male population of the country have gone to the gold district. Our commanding officer [fears that] soldiers cannot be kept in the public service without a large increase in pay."

Everyone wanted to get rich quick. People left their jobs and spent their hard-earned savings to travel to California's goldfields. California's population jumped from 15,000 to 100,000 between 1848 and 1850. At this time, the **nation**'s entire population was 23 million.

▲ When gold nuggets were discovered at John Sutter's sawmill, people swarmed to his land. But he sold off mining rights to the gold too cheaply and, in 1873, he moved to Pennsylvania, bankrupt.

▲ Clipper ships took gold prospectors from New York round South America to San Francisco. This 1851 poster advertises a 100–day voyage on the *Ocean Express*.

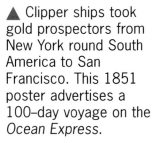

36

▶ A portrait of George W. Northrup, a gold miner of 1849.

▼ Gold miners were also known as prospectors because they were taking a chance and hoping to "strike it lucky." They lived in wooden cabins on the goldfields.

Mixed fortunes on the goldfields

The men and women who joined the 1849 Gold Rush were called forty-niners. Some went to California on ships. Most traveled overland, following the Oregon Trail. Many people in Mexico, China, Australia, and Europe heard about the Gold Rush. They, too, left home for California to try to get rich.

To find gold, forty-niners first went to a stream and used picks to break up the ground. Next, they shoveled mud and gravel into a wooden trough. Then they poured water from the stream into the trough to wash away everything but the gold. A few lucky forty-niners became rich. Most forty-niners found just a little gold, but had to spend it on food and shelter. Discouraged by the Gold Rush, most of them left the goldfields and found other jobs in California.

▲ Gold miners used these tools to pan for gold:
• hammers and pickaxe
• shovels
• water barrel
• bags for gold
• wide metal pans.
The pans were used to swirl around water from the trough, throwing away gravel and leaving the heavy gold at the bottom to pick out.

A Mining Town

Most miners did not get rich in the Gold Rush. Most store owners did. Miners needed food, clothing, tools, and tents. Supplies were low. Demand was high. Many people brought in supplies from the east. They put up a store and charged sky-high prices. Shoes that cost 75 cents in New York cost $8 in California.

Gold and silver mines were discovered in Oregon, Nevada, Wyoming, Montana, California, and Colorado. With each new discovery, people rushed to the site. They left their families at home and promised to come back rich.

Towns sprang up almost overnight. Some miners lived in tents. Others built flimsy shacks. Somebody would open a general store. Another would open a **saloon**. Business would boom. Yet life was far from comfortable. Even water was hard to find. Some people carried it long distances and sold it for lots of money.

▲ The general store sold mining tools, rifles, guns, gunpowder for blasting rock apart, food, clothing, and cooking equipment.

▲ In a mining town, houses and stores were built facing each other. The path down the middle was called Main Street. If it looked as if a town would become permanent, the people built sidewalks out of wooden boards.

◄ These miners were photographed in 1852. The men on the left are from European countries. The men on the right are from China.

38

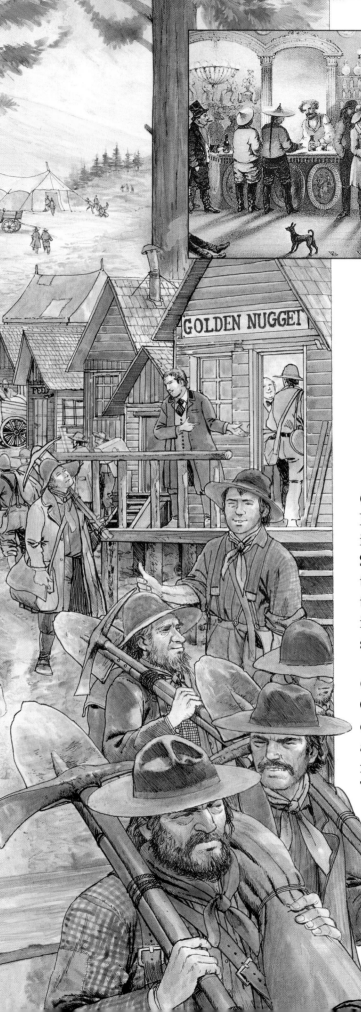

◄ This painting of 1850 shows miners of many nationalities drinking together in a saloon in San Francisco. There were few women in the mining towns because conditions were rough and mining was not considered women's work.

◄ The saloon sold alcoholic drinks such as whiskey, gin, vodka, brandy, and beer. After a hard day's work in the mine, miners often spent their evenings— and most of the their money—in the saloon. Often they got drunk and fights broke out.

Chinese immigrants

Many people came from China to work in the mining towns. Most were miners. Some opened businesses. Others became the cooks and clothes washers for the town. Some Chinese people made money in America and returned home. Most stayed in California.

Ghost towns

Gold and silver are natural resources that cannot be renewed as trees can. As soon as the miners found no more metals in a mine, they abandoned it as worthless. There was no reason for them to stay on the land. They moved on to a more profitable location. Some looked for other goldfields. Most looked for other jobs. Within days, a town could become empty. Then they called it a ghost town.

SNAPSHOT OF AMERICA

By 1850, the United States stretched from Maine on the Atlantic Coast to California on the Pacific Coast. There were over 23 million Americans—20 million more than at the first census in 1790. More people lived in towns and cities than ever before, and more people were moving across the country.

There were many kinds of Americans. There were Native Americans and African Americans. There were people who had fought in the American **Revolution** and people who had just arrived from other countries.

What did these Americans have in common? Generally, Americans believed in looking for a better life and taking risks to find it. They believed in protecting their land and their freedom.

▼ In 1850, there were more than two million **slaves** in America. Many people in the South used slaves to keep their **plantations** working, as shown in this painting of 1861.

▲▶ The numbers on this map show where these settlers set up home. Some Americans stayed on the same land as their grandparents. Others settled in new places. By the 1850s, many of them were arriving in their new communities by railroad and steamship rather than on wagon trains.

1 Chinese settlers came to California to mine for gold and open stores. Many of them stayed in California and helped the state grow.

2 Many Mexican Americans were cowboys. They took care of cattle on ranches in California, Texas, and New Mexico.

3 The Indian Removal Act of 1830 forced all Native Americans to live west of the Mississippi. There, many died of starvation and disease.

Immigrants in America

People who had come from other countries helped America in many ways. Thanks to their skills and energy, they helped factories and farms to grow. **Immigrants** also introduced their music, language, and customs to America. Eggrolls, bagels, and hot dogs were just a few foods that immigrants introduced.

Living in a new land

Many immigrants found a better life. They learned to speak English. They found jobs in cities, or they traveled west and bought land. They wrote letters to friends back in Europe. "Most people eat three meals a day," and "In America, a worker and a government official are regarded as equals," were typical quotes.

◀ Immigrants at New York Harbor, from Frank Leslie's *Illustrated Newspaper* of 1866. The immigrants arrived by ship from Europe. They had to register, or sign official documents, to become citizens. In 1850, over 300,000 European immigrants arrived in America. Their trip took between 40 days and 6 months.

4 Many people came to America from Germany because they could not find work in Germany. Many headed west and became farmers.

5 Many free African Americans became cowboys, **miners**, and factory workers. Most African Americans were slaves in the South.

6 Irish immigrants came to America in the 1840s and 1850s to escape Ireland's potato **famine**. Many worked in factories in the East.

7 Whalers stayed aboard their ships for months at a time. Many of them lived in whaling villages in Connecticut and Massachusetts.

Historical Map of America

ALASKA **CANADA**

Aleutian Islands

PACIFIC OCEAN

On the map

By 1850, nearly the entire mainland of the United States was complete. Only the tiny strip called the Gadsden Purchase was bought in 1853. In 1850, there were 31 states. The rest of the land was divided into territories. Thousands of pioneers left their homes in the East and followed westward trails to California and Oregon Territory.

The Native Americans suffered greatly from the growth of the United States. In 1830, Native Americans were forced to move west of the Mississippi. In 1838, over 15,000 were forced to walk the "Trail of Tears" to Indian Territory.

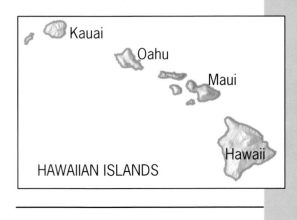

Kauai

Oahu

Maui

Hawaii

HAWAIIAN ISLANDS

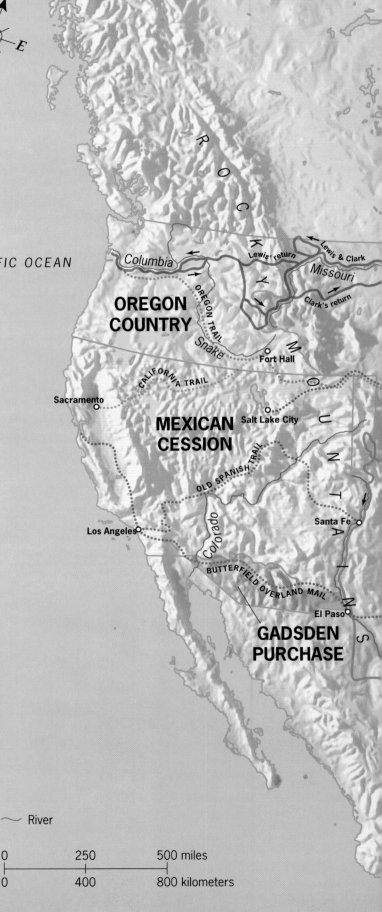

ROCKY MOUNTAINS

Columbia

Lewis' return

Lewis & Clark

Missouri

Clark's return

OREGON COUNTRY

OREGON TRAIL

Snake

Fort Hall

CALIFORNIA TRAIL

Sacramento

Salt Lake City

MEXICAN CESSION

OLD SPANISH TRAIL

Colorado

Santa Fe

Los Angeles

BUTTERFIELD OVERLAND MAIL

El Paso

GADSDEN PURCHASE

~ River

| 0 | 250 | 500 miles |
| 0 | 400 | 800 kilometers |

Hudson Bay

C A N A D A

St. Lawrence

Lake Superior

Pike

Mississippi

Lake Michigan

Lake Huron

Lake Ontario

Erie Canal

Hudson

Lake Erie

Missouri

Lewis & Clark

LOUISIANA PURCHASE

MORMON TRAIL

Dunbar & Hunter

OREGON TRAIL

Council Bluffs

Lewis & Clark

Pike

Independence

St. Louis

Pike

← Pike

INDIANA TERRITORY

OHIO TERRITORY

Delaware

James

UNITED STATES

KENTUCKY

ATLANTIC OCEAN

Ohio

TRAIL OF TEARS

Pike

TENNESSEE

Mississippi

APPALACHIAN MOUNTAINS

13 ORIGINAL STATES

Fort Smith

Arkansas

Mississippi

Dunbar & Hunter

Freeman & Sparks

BUTTERFIELD OVERLAND MAIL

MISSISSIPPI TERRITORY

TEXAS ANNEXATION

FLORIDA

Pike

Rio Grande

MEXICO

GULF OF MEXICO

CARIBBEAN SEA

FAMOUS PEOPLE OF THE TIME

John Quincy Adams, 1767–1848, was the son of President John Adams. He became the sixth U.S. president, serving from 1825 to 1829. His ideas on spending government money on improving roads and farms were not popular.

William Clark, 1770–1838, led the first expedition across the continent with Meriwether Lewis. Later he became governor of the Missouri Territory.

DeWitt Clinton, 1769–1828, carried out plans to build the Erie Canal. He also was mayor of New York City and governor of New York State.

Davy Crockett, 1786–1836, was a symbol of the American frontier. He fought Native Americans to take away their land. He was elected to Congress from Tennessee. When he moved to Texas, he fought at the Alamo and died there.

Millard Fillmore, 1800–1874, was the 13th U.S. president. He stopped a war between the North and South over slavery.

Robert Fulton, 1765–1815, built America's first commercially successful steamboat, the *Clermont*. He also built some of the first submarines, including *Nautilus* in 1798.

William Henry Harrison, 1773–1841, was the ninth president of the United States. He served the shortest term in history: 30 days. He died in the White House of pneumonia.

Samuel Houston, 1793–1863, fought the Mexicans to win independence for Texas. He was the first president of the Republic of Texas. After Texas became a state, he was a senator and then governor of Texas.

Andrew Jackson, 1767–1845, was the seventh U.S. president. He wanted more ordinary people to participate in government. Yet he helped to force all Native Americans to move west of the Mississippi River.

Thomas Jefferson, 1743–1826, played an important role in starting the United States. As the third U. S. president, he requested the Lewis and Clark expedition.

Meriwether Lewis, 1774–1809, led the first expedition across the continent with William Clark. Later he became governor of the Louisiana Territory.

James Madison, 1751–1836, was the fourth U.S. president. When he entered the United States in the War of 1812, he was unpopular.

IMPORTANT DATES AND EVENTS

WILLIAM CLARK
1770 born in Caroline County, Virginia
1789 fights battles against Native Americans in Indiana and Kentucky
1796 resigns from the military
1803 accepts invitation to make expedition across the continent with Meriwether Lewis
1804 begins the journey on May 14 from St. Louis
1805 reaches the Pacific Ocean on November 7
1806 returns to St. Louis on September 23
1808 marries Julia Hancock
1813 appointed governor of Missouri Territory
1821 married Harriet Kennerly after his first wife died
1825 worked on peace treaties with Native Americans
1838 died in St. Louis on September 1

MERIWETHER LEWIS
1774 born in Albemarle County, Virginia
1794 joins the U.S. Army
1801 becomes private secretary to President Thomas Jefferson
1803 begins planning expedition across the continent with William Clark
1804 begins the journey on May 14 from St. Louis
1805 reaches the Pacific Ocean on November 7
1806 returns to St. Louis on September 23
1807 appointed governor of Louisiana Territory
1809 died on October 11 [Historians say he either committed suicide or was murdered.]

EVENTS OF THE BOOK
1793 Eli Whitney invents the cotton gin
1801 Thomas Jefferson becomes president
1803 Louisiana Purchase
1804–1806 Lewis and Clark make their expedition
1807 *The Clermont*, the first profitable steamboat, is launched
1809 James Madison becomes president
1812 War of 1812 begins
1814 British burn the White House and other government buildings in Washington, D.C.
1814 The War of 1812 ends
1814 Francis Lowell builds America's first factory, a cotton mill
1817 James Monroe becomes president
1819 U.S. buys Florida from Spain
1825 John Quincy Adams becomes president
1825 the Erie Canal is completed

Cyrus McCormick, 1809–1884, invented a reaper that helped farmers cut wheat in the fields.

James Monroe, 1758–1831, helped negotiate the Louisiana Purchase. He became the fifth president of the United States in 1817. During his term, the U.S. purchased Florida from Spain.

Osceola, 1800?–1838, was a leader of the Seminole Native Americans. He fought the U.S. government when they tried to move the Seminoles out of Florida.

Oliver Perry, 1785–1819, was a navy officer in the War of 1812. His victory in the battle for Lake Erie was an important turning point in the war against Britain.

James Polk, 1795–1849, was the 11th president of the United States. During his term (1845–1849), the U.S. won the Mexican War and acquired California and the Southwest.

Sacagawea, 1786–1812?, was a Native American and the only woman on the Lewis and Clark expedition. She served as a guide and language interpreter with the Shoshone tribe.

Antonio Lopéz de Santa Anna, 1794–1876, was the leader of Mexico when Texas fought for independence.

John Sutter, 1803–1880, started a settlement in California. Gold was discovered near his sawmill in 1848. Miners swarmed to his land the following year, creating the Gold Rush.

Zachary Taylor, 1785–1850, was a hero of the Mexican War. He became the 12th president of the United States in 1849. He died in office after serving one year and four months.

Tecumseh, 1768?–1813, was a Shawnee chief. He led his people against the U.S. government as they tried to keep their land. He died in the War of 1812, fighting for the British.

John Tyler, 1790–1862, was the tenth president of the United States. He was the first vice president to take over the presidency when President Harrison died. He served from 1841 to 1845.

Martin Van Buren, 1782–1862, was the eighth U.S. president. He was president from 1837 to 1841, during an economic depression. He ran for president two more times and lost on each occasion.

Eli Whitney, 1765–1825, invented the cotton gin in 1793 which separated cotton seeds from the fiber.

Brigham Young, 1801–1877, led people of the Mormon religion to Salt Lake City, Utah. He headed the Mormon church there and was briefly governor of the Utah Territory.

? means that historians are not sure of the exact date

EVENTS OF THE BOOK CONTINUED
1829 Andrew Jackson becomes president
1830 Indian Removal Act
1832 McCormick invents reaper
1835–1839 Trail of Tears
1835–1842 U.S. Army fights the Seminoles in Florida
1835 fire burns 700 buildings in New York City
1836 Texas wins independence from Mexico
1837 Martin Van Buren becomes president
1841 William H. Harrison becomes president
1841 John Tyler becomes president
1845 James Polk becomes president
1845 Texas joins the United States
1846–1848 U.S. at war with Mexico
1847 Mormons reach Utah
1848 Mexican Cession
1848 Oregon becomes a territory of the United States
1849 Zachary Taylor becomes president
1849 California Gold Rush
1850 Millard Fillmore becomes president
1853 Gadsden Purchase

THE REST OF AMERICA
1810 Argentina declares independence from Spain
1811 Paraguay and Venezuela declare independence from Spain
1812–1815 British and Canadian forces stop U.S. invasion of eastern Canada
1813 Colombia declares independence from Spain
1814 Uruguay declares independence from Spain
1818 Chile, led by Simón Bolívar, gains independence from Spain
1821 Mexico, El Salvador, and Costa Rica win independence from Spain
1822 Brazil gains independence from Portugal
1838–1840 Honduras, Nicaragua, and Guatemala become independent from Spain
1841 The Act of Union joins Upper and Lower Canada into the Province of Canada

THE REST OF THE WORLD
1801–1850 start of British dominance in India and the Far East
1804 Briton Richard Trevithick makes the first steam train
1807 slave trade abolished in the British Empire
1807 Sierra Leone and Gambia become British colonies
1812 French army led by Napoleon Bonaparte invades Russia
1819 Singapore is founded by Britain
1826 photography invented
1826–1828 Russia and Persia at war. Russia gains Armenia.
1839 New Zealand becomes a British colony
1842–1847 British and Dutch at war in South Africa
1848 revolutions in Italy, France, Austria, and Germany

GLOSSARY

abolitionist person who is against slavery

ambush hiding in order to attack by surprise

boardinghouse house where meals and a sleeping room are provided for pay

boundary border; dividing line between two countries

census count of the number of people in a country

Congress branch of the U.S. government that makes laws

constitution set of laws that state the rights of the people and the power of the government

corset garment worn by women under a dress to shape the body

election process of choosing someone by voting

engraving artwork made by cutting into metal, wood, or glass surface

equality condition of being equal, especially having equal rights and responsibilities

extinct all types have died out

famine serious lack of food

frontier land between a settled area and wilderness

Great Plains land between the Mississippi River and the Rocky Mountains. It is mostly grassland or prairie.

harpoon pointed spear with a rope attached to it

House of Burgesses representative government in colonial Virginia

immigrant someone who moves from another country

kerosene colorless fuel made from petroleum (oil found below the Earth's surface)

lithograph print made from a flat stone or metal plate

military having to do with soldiers or war

miner person who digs in the earth to get out precious stones, gold, coal, and other valuable resources

mill building with machines for processing cloth or grinding grain to make flour

mission settlement of religious teachers, including a church and other buildings

nation the community of people within a country, usually sharing the same territory and government

peddler person who travels from place to place, selling things

pioneer person who does something first, like settling in a new area, to make it easier for others to follow

plantation large farm where often cotton or tobacco are grown

representative someone who acts and speaks for people as laws are made

revolution complete change, as a change from hand crafting to manufacturing by machines, or in gaining independence from another country

saloon place where alcoholic drinks are sold

secretary of state leading member of the U.S. government's state department. The department handles relationships with other governments.

Senate one of the two groups in Congress that makes laws for the United States

slave person who is owned by another person and is usually made to work for that person

state one of the parts of a nation. In the U.S., each state has its own government and laws.

territory in the United States, an area that is not yet a state

trading post place where people trade goods with people who live in the area

treaty written agreement between two countries, usually to prevent or end a war

tribe group of people who share a territory, language, customs, and laws

wagon train group of covered wagons that traveled to the West together

HISTORICAL FICTION TO READ

Beatty, Patricia. *How Many Miles to Sundown?* New York: Morrow, 1974. A 13-year-old girl follows her brother and a friend into Texas, Mexico, and Arizona during the 1800s to look for the friend's father.

Byars, Betsy. *Trouble River.* New York: Viking, 1969. Twelve-year-old Dewey and his grandmother end up traveling 40 miles (64 km) down Trouble River on his homemade raft to avoid hostile Native Americans when their cabin is threatened.

O'Dell, Scott. *Streams to the River, River to the Sea: A Novel of Sacajawea.* New York: Houghton, 1986. Tells the story of the Lewis and Clark expedition through the eyes of the young Shoshone woman who served as interpreter and often guide.

Woodruff, Elvira. *Dear Levi: Letters from the Overland Trail.* New York. Knopf, 1994. Twelve-year-old Austin writers letters to his brother as he travels from Sudbury, Pennsylvania, to Oregon in 1850.

HISTORIC SITES TO VISIT

Jefferson National Expansion Memorial
11 N. Fourth Street, St. Louis, MO 63102
Telephone: (314) 425-6010 This park commemorates the westward expansion of the United States and the settlement of St. Louis. It includes the Gateway Arch that symbolizes St. Louis as the "Gateway to the West."

Mystic Seaport
The Museum of America and the Sea
75 Greenmanville Avenue, P.O. Box 6000,
Mystic, CT 06355 Telephone: (888)732-7678
This re-created seaport whaling village shows what life was like in the 19th century. It includes an 156-year-old whaleship, stores, and craftworkers.

The Alamo
300 Alamo Plaza, San Antonio, TX 78205
Telephone: (210) 225-1391
Once a Spanish mission, then an American fort, the Alamo is a monument to the U.S. volunteers who died in 1836 in Texas's fight for independence from Mexico.

Wind River Indian Reservation
Shoshone Cultural Center
P.O. Box 538, Fort Washakie, WY 82514
Telephone: (307) 332-9106 Shoshone and Arapaho tribes live on this reservation. Sacagawea is buried here. Native Americans from around the country gather here for celebrations, called powwows.

Wayne County Historical Society Museum
810 Main Street, Honesdale, PA 18431
Telephone: (717) 253-3240.
The museum includes historical features of the Delaware and Hudson Canal Company. There is also a replica of the *Stourbridge Lion*, the first steam locomotive used in the United States.

INDEX

INDEX